Orpheus the Healer

"Unlike the human failure that ripped the mythological Orpheus to pieces, V. B. Price defiantly offers his head so the reader can stare victoriously back at our collective crossroads. His opus *Orpheus the Healer* treads through the restlessness that drives us when we are on the brink, ambushed by feelings of unworthiness and insecurity. His lament, best savored out loud, is an intoxicating soul dance—alive, spontaneous and free—in which the need for answers has passed from his world. This must-read literary journey proffers the ultimate human gift of how to release the fear of the unknown and hold onto the beauty of life beyond that which we think we know."

—ANNA C. MARTINEZ,
author of PURA PUTA: A POETIC MEMOIR,
City of Albuquerque Poet Laureate Emerita

"*Orpheus the Healer* is a full-throated gift from V. B. Price. It's as if this mature collection was struggling to emerge from his pen and was finally made possible by a series of traumatic and then miraculous events in rapid succession.... The mysterious synchronicity of these events gave birth to *Orpheus the Healer,* and I believe readers will agree it is the poet's finest work to date. Read this book and revel in creativity and hope."

—MARGARET RANDALL,
author of LAST WORDS

"A most intimate exploration of grief, loss, and the kaleidoscope of memory. The Orphic way unlocks the secrets of gratitude to those with the courage to deeply survey the history of self and its relational fiber. V. B. Price shows us that the power of poetry is its process—to mourn, examine, and eventually heal."

—BENITO ARAGON,
publisher and co-founder of
NEW MEXICO MERCURY

ORPHEUS
the HEALER
and other poems

V. B. Price

Casa Urraca Press
ABIQUIÚ

Original cover photograph by V. B. Price,
    of the cairn he made for Rini Price upon her death.

Author photographs by Magdalena Lily McCarson.

Set in Krete and Sirenne.

28 27 26 25   1 2 3 4 5 6 7

First edition

ISBN 978-1-956375-37-4

CASA URRACA PRESS

an imprint of Casa Urraca, Ltd.
PO Box 1119
Abiquiú, New Mexico 87510
casaurracapress.com

For Robin,
because she asked me to tell her
more about Rini.

In Memoriam

Rini Price
Bill Swift

"Poetry is a form of power. It fell to early thought to make that power visible and human, and the story of Orpheus is that vision and that mortality."

—Elizabeth Sewell,
The Orphic Voice

THE ELEGIAC NATURE OF THE POEMS IN THIS BOOK reflects on the underlying and ever-present reality of loss and grief in all our lives. The gradual and unstoppable accumulation of the deaths of friends and family, and the vacancy and longing they leave behind, is as close to a universal human condition, and a particularly cruel condition of aging, as anything could be. If you live long enough, it's entirely possible you'll become orphaned from all the important relationships of your life, even those you thought you could never live without. If you're lucky, sometimes a new community evolves with new friends, even new loves, and with your own children and grandchildren and former students becoming part of your developing inner circle. The jagged sense of being exiled in the future and left behind by the past might soften with time, but it does not seem ever to go away. It can leave many of us feeling painfully haunted and abandoned for the rest of our lives. Oddly, such ubiquitous feelings do not seem to bind us in a comforting global community of people who understand empathetically the impact of loss. Rather, we appear to be further isolated in our griefs, regrets, resentments, and tribal connections.

It is out of such a context that this book of poems appeared over the last four or five years. It is divided into three sections, "Orpheus the Healer," "Emotion," and "Rio Grande Elegies." The first section uses the myth of the god of poetry as a map to the rending of a tragic loss and the futility of efforts to try to repair it, even superficially, defying the ironclad laws of life and death. The Orpheus poems explore whether it's possible to uncover some of the bare bones of a universal story of grief and denial, and the homesickness left in the wake of the untimely death of intimates. It sees the grief of Orpheus as an extreme on one end of a spectrum. The other end of the spectrum is murderous, null indifference.

The second section works to connect the personal with the universal through the medium of feelings often experienced and endured but too seldom treated as pressing realities worthy of exploration in themselves.

The third section, and the most personal, celebrates the spirit of my late wife, the artist Rini Price, as well as some of the lives of a large and growing community of deceased friends and family who populate my mythology of the past, a world that remains in the history of time but is no longer able to adapt and evolve. The Elegy poems explore the idiosyncratic and the unreplaceable. They are forms of lamentation. Each elegy is about someone who was a part of the structural underpinning of my existence. I haven't collapsed from their passings, but I will always feel destabilized without them. As the old Anglo Saxon scop would say, "age under ate them"— and under ate me.

The myth of Orpheus gives us a way to start structuring the flow of life and loss that runs through all our histories. Its lessons are for each of us to discover. The myth itself has been spun in many ways. For the sake of clarity, I include my version of the myth as follows:

Orpheus is an early Greek deity from the mysterious hinterlands of Thrace. Poetry, "music wedded to language," falls under his

patronage and protection. Fragments of myth have it that
Orpheus accompanied Jason and the Argonauts on their voyage
to retrieve the Golden Fleece, helping the crew evade the deadly
charms of the Sirens and their crashing rocks by outsinging them
with his melodious and poetic magic. He next appears in many
representations performing with all of nature gathered around
him, listening intently and moving joyously—trees, birds and
beasts, even rocks, even mountains. He delights the world and
the world feels loved by him, a love that takes the form of its own
self-knowledge amplified and deepened through his praising voice.
But when Orpheus falls in love with Eurydice—whose name
means "wide justice"—and marries her, all misfortune, it seems,
comes to haunt him in retribution for his perfect love. While
walking through a meadow full of wildflowers and bees, Eurydice
finds herself being chased by an unknown man and, fearful of
rape, pays no attention to the venomous snake ahead. She steps
on it and it bites her foot. Nothing can save her, not even Orpheus
and his healing voice. And she is taken down to the land of Hades,
never to return. But Orpheus loves her so much, he cannot bear
his grief. He defies the finality of death and takes the journey, a
katabasis, into the underworld to plead with Hades to do what
he has never done—to let Eurydice go back to the world alive
and whole. Orpheus sings with such a beautiful passion that he
charms the god into doing the unthinkable, with one condition:
yes, Eurydice can return to Orpheus in the fullness of her youth;
but, if he looks back at her before she reaches life again, she will be
cast back into the clutches of the dead. Orpheus cannot resist the
temptation and, as Hades must have known he would, glances
back as he nears the surface. What he sees he cannot bear—
Eurydice falling back into the holy darkness forever. Orpheus's
grief and horror overwhelm him. His lamenting is unstoppable.
He refuses all comfort and condolence. He allows no one near him.
Eventually, his refusal of all overtures of love comes to infuriate
the wild and beautiful followers of Dionysus, god of energy,
imagination, drama, and wine. In a frenzy, they grab Orpheus
and tear him apart. His severed head keeps singing its sweet

tragedy as it is carried away on the tides. His grief turns his song into prophesy, and his singing head eventually lands on the Isle of Lesbos. There, he continues to make prophetic utterances until, finally, Apollo, god of oracles, makes him stop with the promise that his lyre will be taken by an eagle into the heavens and turned into the five-starred constellation Lyra, whose largest star, Vega, is often the brightest star in the sky.

Orpheus works to heal himself through the internal processing that poetry allows. In keeping with what Viktor Frankl calls "paradoxical intention," Orpheus tries so hard to heal that he ceases to be a healer; he denies the comfort and love of others who have processed grief themselves. The healing process is thwarted by the psychological scab of narcissism, which forces grief to fester and turns a whole life into an incurable and lamentable sepsis, beyond the help of anything or anyone.

The myth tells us that being unable to lift yourself out of ceaseless lamentation can turn grief into a psychological dismembering, leaving you at the mercy of the self-devouring forces of emotional entropy. This state of mind can descend ultimately to an inner collapse in which your life itself rejects you as being too painful for it to bear. You are abandoned again, this time by your own ambitions and love of life. It is a lethal situation, for it closes you off to all the other wonders, beauties, meanings, and blessings of the world. In fact, it makes the saving grace of gratitude for your own life impossible. And without gratitude there is little else to live for.

ORPHEUS *the* HEALER

ALL OF US MUST BE POETS,
some with poems, and some

without. All of us
live the Orphic way.

It's a pattern,
a first infatuation

with the world,
world as goodness,

world as soul. Orpheus
sang the gulls diving,

the trees swaying,
the flowers in their

ditties and symphonies.
Then the Great Love

finds him, and almost at
the same moment he

begins to notice, unnamed,
entropy advancing. And

he is reborn,
even for a moment

or what seems
a whole life long,

and he sings this love
through the world.

And then
she dies.

He, like us,
encounters death

in his heart,
in his teeth

and tries to foil it
with futile bargaining.

He looks back on what
he loved and loses her

again, and as
we do, we see

entropy advance,
poets silent or

breathing meaning,
watching the obscene

Anthropocene chew
and grind itself to paste

from which no
new life is ever born.

We escape
to sing

our way away,
as far as life

will let us say,
and then succumb,

scattered by
the tearing gravity

of grief we've asked
the world to bear with us

holding off the
flood gates

until now when
everything is gone.

WHAT DID ORPHEUS SING
to the rocks and trees,

the beasts, the land, the clouds?
What did his singing

head foretell when death's
madness tore him to shreds?

What were the words
he sang to Hades that let

the greedy Him relent
and let her go back

to the world, if Orpheus
and his great will could hold

out against the devil's deal?
They were not the words that Ovid

put in his mouth to spit out.
What was his lament?

How did it sound?
What words did he choose?

What is missing
is translation.

Everything is
translation,

some glimpse
of the geode cave

from which all song,
all thought, all self emerges.

That glimpse is not for us
to have, as the wise

doctor said. I cannot
experience your experience,

only your behavior.
If you don't say,

I cannot hear you, cannot
hear what only you can hear.

All our powers are
hearsay only. Orpheus must

have sung poems in
hellacious melodies

Hades could translate.
He must have formed

His sorrow into admiration's
Siren song, praise come alive,

melodies played on the instrument
of charcoal trees, black windrows.

But what were the lyrics?
What did he say?

Not the Orphic scripture, surely,
with its mad judgments, but

punishment might
turn Hades on, sorrow

delicious to the sadist,
locked doors burning

far below. Or did he sing
I knew her naked warm from bed.

*I knew her with wine
in our garden, geraniums*

*red with her delight.
I knew her by the Christmas fire*

*with eggs and bacon, piles of presents.
Do you remember how that felt?*

And now she is gone, nowhere
but here with you. It must

have been cosmically
better than that. But

what? Is that his
ultimate lament,

our ultimate lament,
that all we are is

unknowable,
untranslatable because

we are unsaid,
unsayable?

WHEN YOU SING
your lament to the devil,

you think the beast is
listening to what you

have to say. But his
hearing aids record

your voice as his own, so
he hears himself talking

and saying things he thinks
are jokes and says them back

and you take them for
admonitions—*don't*

look back, and, of course,
when he says that, you

must disobey. You can't
help yourself, and you lose

again. This time
everything again, in grief

for what you could
not help, like falling

in friendship with
a person who has no

social sense, no empathy,
a person your sense

of rudeness warns you
not to turn your back on.

But you do the opposite
again, and lose the angel

of your self-regard
for a moment, wasting

your time trying to get
a warm response from

an echoing stone
misconceiving.

IT IS YOU
who sings

the ten thousand things,
the infinite unfolding,

life's order
from death's disorder

in decline, rich
as the loam of time.

You are the song
that changes itself

to sing the world
back into life.

You were that
song before doubt

corrupted praise.
Even before, in the ancient

childhood before death,
you learned

to sing the unfurling
when the world moves

to your melody. Praise
connects, blooms

with how the cosmos
plays itself out in its

ever-vast wild bounty
as when you feel your

whole being momentarily
transformed by a breezy

summer morning, or
by the symphonic dawn

of an insight epiphany
of all being as it must be,

including you. When you
learn the instrument

of the world, learn to
play the world, its music

is your voice in harmony
with time, with your

praising heart, with
poems as natural as wind

playing the leaves,
the whole forest,

playing light
through clouds,

playing moon
through tides,

playing days
and daylessness

beyond our sun,
playing and being

played upon by galaxies'
fathomless plenty unfolding

like ferns or arrays
of gladiolas bursting

mysterious, adored,
unknown as words

before they're born,
strummed and sung.

WE KNOW, MORE
than any specialist,

what happens when
you let the spirit,

the universe, speak
through you on the page

in words you can
grasp, or in a forest

grove given to dancing
to your melodies.

We know the complexity
of the invisible

chaos of being
playing us like wind

plays grass and ocean
lulling, rippling surfaces

to give them meaning.
We cannot know how,

nor can we say exactly
what. But the followers

of Orpheus know all
there is to know about

emergence. Every poem is
emergent, appearing

out of the unfurling
"generative force" that is

the Tao, the Cosmos
at its heart,

operating without
scripts known to us,

known to me. How do
poems emerge from my brain?

I don't know, but I know
how it feels when they do.

Is that one step closer
to knowing a living

Theory of the Mystery?
The brittle miniaturists

of physics would laugh.
How can they measure

mere feeling
in elements?

A poem, though, is
the essence of Mystery

as love, as good luck,
are. Not only what

the poem says, but that
it has appeared at all.

The saying belongs to another step up
beyond appearance,

too much, itself, to say
or mean through and through

beyond the intent to receive it
and read it first.

THE POET AND THE WARRIORS
went off on a dare in ships,

to sack and kill and swarm
and have their infamy portrayed

as hero stuff, beyond reproach.
They voyaged beyond the pale

of safety and the worrisome loss
of comforts. Apollo's bird,

the poet, sang beauty
from order, lulled

the crashing rocks
and strummed the dragon

drowsy. The Golden
Fleece was theirs.

And the Argo, strong
and slick, could sail

and Jason meet his fate.
Orpheus was no

fellow traveler, scribe,
waiting and witnessing

so he could describe
the fury and festivities

of mayhem. He was there
and his song was a consoling

weapon, the start, perhaps,
the mythic source

of speech as persuasion,
deceit, compulsion and

false will doing evil
in the long-sung

fields of glory. Perhaps
Apollo's breath is

a secret bomb
of calm and stillness,

perhaps that was
the beginning of his

fateful loss and dazed
dismemberment, Orpheus

as a god, but not
too frail to be in ruins.

WATCHING HER SUFFER,
helpless, she who you cannot be

who you are without;
the conqueror making you watch

the torture of your children,
Hades released in full

malignancy, and you
go after him, begging

while memory does its tricks,
the stone that feels cool

as her hand, her shadow
on the wall behind the big tree,

a gust of her turning
into the bedroom

down the hall. You feel
her, and you turn

and as you recognize
the feeling, it's as if

it never was. The devil's trick
of warning you not to know,

it makes you helpless
to the knowing again

all over and gone,
and all that's left of you

is you alone, trying to keep
being who you are without

going mad and being rendered,
butchered by the furies

of grief and guilt and regret
and abject uselessness

in the face of the way
it is and will always be

from now until the end,
a life ruled by a without,

being more than a vacancy,
a sweet joy never to be

known again. But you
cannot stop howling

and the neighbors want
you silenced and are

going mad themselves
with their own jaws of loss.

And you are banished
to your loneliness,

once more, not the loss
of your first home, not

the divorce, but the loss
of everything that healed

your homesick dread
and replaced it with

open arms and the
safety of a life ahead.

HE KNEW IF SHE
could die, like a bee

in a spider trap, killed
by accident but on purpose

by the spider, if she
could die then reason,

hope, meaning all
seemed at the end

of their unraveling.
If *she* could die then

what is most precious
to us means nothing

to the way things are.
And the only antidote

the poet had was
the counterpoint

of praise and
beauty which

themselves are
fragile as dry

grass is to sparks
in a breeze.

The lament
of flame, this

is what he wailed:
the meaning of meaning

means nothing—the
final snicker of what

is fated only because
it has happened to happen.

THE SOUL OF ORPHEUS
is the knowledge that

singing makes it so, that
what you think

to yourself and say
to yourself makes real

what is, that you can see it
however you wish

and however you do is real,
not necessarily true. You are

free to make your world, free
to live the meaning

that you make. Some
brave ones may say

and do on their own.
Most of us need

authority to tell us
what is real, even if

authority is
a myth that you

yourself have supposed
to be true. This all

takes a certain
gullibility—I was

about to say
"innocent gullibility."

But the myth you suppose
must leave you with the feeling

it is so true that to ignore
or deny it would be a folly

worthy of the auto-
annihilation of

self-disgust, and
the destruction

of your self-respect,
that you would

always, as a skeptic,
come to the edge

of incredulity
and immediately step

back, if you were in
your right mind.

Orpheus must have
sung that freedom,

his half-god's knowing
of it. And the song

came to everything
with the force of truth

revealed and practiced,
so even the god of hell

partially buckled.
We are what we tell

ourselves we are.
The world is

as we say it
and refine it

and redraft it
and hear it

spoken back to us
in our own voice. A billion

makers of reality
can't be all wrong.

ORPHEUS WAS
an enthusiast.

He loved and
praised all out.

He loathed
and wept all out.

The song that moved
the trees and rattled

the Devil was a
song of inconsolable

praise. He missed
nothing. His wonder

made the rocks
and trees feel so

good about themselves
they danced for joy

when he sang
them—just as a lover

feels the glory
of being truly loved

and truly loving—
the rule of life

that puts your life
in your own hands

every bit as much
as your helplessness

to what is
determines

the landscape
of your living.

People sink
into their habits,

their fear, their
greed, and find

enthusiasts to be
phonies—"methinks

he doth protest
too much." And they

may rip us apart
for the enthusiasm

of our suffering
and our grief,

leaving us only
a singing head

prophesying
the obvious. Still,

better that than
to have the world

fall dead at
the thought of us!

NEVER CLOSE
yourself off to love.

If you do,
you will be ripped

apart by those
who would love you,

by the furious animas
and fascinations of

the future you have
rejected before it

even had a chance
to want you, and now

the gaping future
devours you, you are

your sullen, suicidal,
constipated grief

for what is not, for
what can never be

again. And so what
could be, what might be,

revenge themselves upon you
with your own mind

the conduit of their
rage at the loss

of you, those saviors.
Strengthening to love

again is rolling
away the stone,

is silencing your own
singing head as it

rolls over the cliff
to the rocks below.

GILGAMESH AND ENKIDU
slaying Humbaba

in his forest, a song
Orpheus sang

in cuneiform when
he was first able

to find an instrument
he could play.

He strummed the tall
charcoal trees,

the clear-cut stubble,
as he would pluck

wheat chaff into
symphonies of breezes

and lush swaying,
cleaning the air,

cleaning the lungs
of the God so he could

always sing afresh
in others. Orpheus

will do that again,
through us, pluck the

ruins of humanity, play
the waste, practice the keys

and strings and reeds
of the fallen end.

It is for us, through
the Orphic voice, to make

a body of song
that does not waste

at least this
ultimate wastefulness

that we have
turned out to be.

DID HE KNOW
what he was lamenting,

beyond his own dismembering
loss? What crushing

truth did he feel
that he didn't feel

before, what moved
him from exuberance

to mourning so much
deeper than complaint?

Was it the injustice
of her death, her twice

dying, once to venom,
once to the betrayal of forgetting?

Do we always lose
what we love at least

thrice, once in dread,
once before our eyes, once

in recollection vanishing?
Lost, the lament of fate,

of accident, of the way it is.
The lament of one

who minds and who
makes a difference,

unwilling to not
be consumed for a while

by the seasickness
of grief. How can he

lament what is, what
his choice could not

contravene? Something so
far beyond the effect

he was, not cause,
but consequence.

Could he be lamenting his
hopeless ignorance, the

blind spots of our species,
could he see the final

sunsets of the
angiosperms,

the world wilting,
boiling, mushing

into soggy rust like
leaves discoloring

the lake of fun
where robins splashed

and bathed? Was his
lament about feeling

silly about lamenting
anything at all?

SINGING THROUGH
the corpses, playing

bones, strumming
ribs, whistling through

skulls, eye sockets,
nose hole stops, Orpheus

harmonizing the Anthropocene,
finding the ringing tones

in glasses filled with
oily water, radioactive

sludge, distilled jet fuel
in the baby's bottle, a drop

or two of rare pure water
in a shallow dish.

The songs of Orpheus,
love notes to the forests

and blossoming of weeds,
to bees, and wasps, and deer,

bear and vultures, his endless
lament, the mourning

howl the god of changes,
"the Wild God of the World,"

hates to hear. After all,
all the gods must do

is everything, and everything
changes, changes, changes.

When the gods change
the world, Orpheus praises,

when humans tear up
the plans, Orpheus

won't relent
in his dirge.

But aren't we
a species too,

don't we do
what we do

as dragonflies do,
as lemurs, yeasts,

dogs and cats
do? Can we

help it? Aren't
we the animal

who thinks it is
better than it is,

convinced it is
virtuous and that

it could change
itself to survive

itself, like too
many sperm whales

refusing to mate
so they won't clog

up the ocean might,
or a beach full of

tarantulas rushing
in hordes to sea

so she can walk
on the sand without

a thought of the
screaming mimmies?

We can change.
We can adapt.

But can we adapt
enough, can we?

We can't turn
ourselves into a

different kind of
energy. Would even

that be enough
at this moment

where plans are
melting and truth

tightens like
barbed wire

that we don't
have enough

breath to
untangle?

Would Orpheus
lament what

cannot not
be?

DID ORPHEUS LAMENT
his ignorance—how much

he didn't know, couldn't
know, would never know—

was that his lament?
His ignorance led him

to be duped
by the tricky

god of death—
always sudden,

surprising,
on purpose,

out of the blue,
sullen, downtrodden

Death tricked him
with a fantasy

a need for proof
he couldn't help

but feel, looking back
his final agency

to lose her, lose
it all, everything

forever. His state
of mind, bad faith,

distrusting death,
knowing it would

never relent as
the only rule—

what starts
ends, always.

Was he dissing
The Divine Enforcer

of the Kingdom
of the Gone? Was he

so stupid as to try
and trick a god,

or was it just
a fatal reflex like

blinking this intrinsic
mistrust? Hadn't the rocks

and trees and beasts
taught him anything?

Ask and ye shall
receive, but always

with Divine strings
tangling the works.

Was he lamenting
his inadequacy,

the inherent
insufficiency of words?

NEUROTIC ORPHIC
impulse, the need

to love and be loved
exactly as you need it,

without any
deviation from

how you have
envisioned it, and

anything different
leads you to doubt

your being loved
at all, that you will

be expelled
at some moment,

relieved of the
relationship, orphaned

from love, the fear
you've had all your life,

being only half a god,
all too human, the same

terrors you felt
as a child, abandoned

into helplessness, into
the worst state of

homesickness,
with only yourself

to hear your lament,
a mandatory introversion

you did not choose. Didn't
you know your lover

needed most of all
your trust? Trust

in her love, trust
in her strength?

Was the backward
glance, your doubt,

your suspicion,
your fatal flaw?

HE WAS FREE,
we hope, to sing

what he wanted,
and he wanted to tell

the things of the world
they are worthy

of song, of hymns
and odes, and lullabies

of praise. He wanted
to sing: "You are perfect

in our struggle
for *the*

perfection of survival.
You are

just by being fit
for being who you are

fit for being
alive, animate

or inanimate, and
as all being is free

of not being,
its freedom must

include action and
mistake and winning

and working." And he
sang all, all that is

perfect in its imperfection too.
He knew that rocks and birds

were some of the stuff
that was enough

for all his praise.
And praise makes

the world dance,
even those who

are sunk in the fear
of being unpraiseworthy.

Orpheus sings them.
We are all

worth the love
of a song.

SINGING BEYOND
the single

principal
reality

of what is,
Orpheus transgressed

the boundary between
is and not,

coaxing the keeper
of the rule of death—

no dead thing can be
reassembled into life again

and be alive
—coaxing him to

subvert his own law,
Orpheus himself was

tricked by the illusion
of his experience. Hades'

hex—*trust, resist, don't*
look back—was the way

the law was preserved,
kept real, once and for all,

affirming humans are
of the same stuff as

everything else,
ruled by the same

rules and cannot
coax reality

to ever become
what it is not.

Orpheus, the god
of the flow of mind

that knows all is
one, but can never

know how
altogether or why

.... The eternal gap
that consciousness

cannot cross,
cannot feel.

Don't look back
was the way

the Mystery
assured itself we

could never
find out,

could never persuade
the truth we can never

understand to become
a trick that fools us

into thinking we
can. The joke is

finally always
on us.

ORPHEUS IN EDEN;
he is not a fallen god.

He did not fall
for power, not an

Adam, and Eurydice
not an Eve. No temptation

until the end, and he,
of course, succumbed.

He had no choice. The god
of All Over had willed it.

Orpheus was tricked and lost
himself to the sleight of mind

of loving too much—
not fallen just mistaken

and tripped up,
not expelled just slipping

on a banana peel,
trying too hard for perfection

and defining himself
by a cheap mistake

and her by the fate of being
loved so much beyond doubt,

a tic of uncertainty
stopped her cold.

ORPHEUS COULD TALK
the hell out of death

for a moment; he calmed
the beasts the Argonauts

faced in the straits at sea.
Song is irresistible—marching

music, lullabies, odes
to joy, they move

mountains, might even
move a horse

standing on your foot,
or be as sinister as

a million scuttling legs
of tarantulas

on a black sand beach
in a sliver of moonlight.

Orpheus is more
than just a voice.

He sings what he means
and what he means is

that beauty has a purpose.
It matters like eyes.

She of the vanishing
and falling back, lived

to make the beautiful
a regular part of everything

that was with her. That
is why Orpheus

risked hell for her.
Hell is the absence

of the inspiration
of pleasure.

BEFORE YOU CAN SING
the trees, the rocks,

or rhumba like the sea,
the birds, the bees, the bears,

you must have been
inspired by what they are

on their own without you—
admiring god, divine devotee,

master of appreciation and
awestruck wonder. You must

have felt the sunny breezes
from the beach play you like

you play the wind, violining
through tall grasses, or hum

water on water as
you orchestrate agate

slabs in a garden acequia
so the dullness of stone

radiates with revealing
light. Orpheus is the god

of praise as poetry is
the instrument of loving

and of being swept away
by the beauty of all others.

That is the background
of the God's loving fire,

the flaming praise
that sets the world

alight and makes
our days God-sent.

ORPHEUS MEANS,
is the metaphor for,

causing the impossible.
When he sings, world

things can't contain
themselves, or refrain

from animation. Wild-
hearted, feral things

with horns and fangs
and claws, wings,

whiskers, beaks,
pause, listen, and

nod ascent. Orpheus
means language as

magic, as beauty with
super-factual powers,

rising above what normally
is without it. When we speak

to ourselves, we can change
even our most inanimate

habits, when we speak out loud
we might, most rarely, change

the habits of others—surely
a metaphor in itself for the

impossibility of strumming such
a catchy tune that boulders are compelled

to dance with sequoias.
Does that

happen to us?
Metaphorically, surely,

if you learn
to accompany

the orchestra of the leaves
and blowing pebbles.

ORPHEUS SINGS THROUGH
us all, the masters, the students,

the mute, sings in a voice
that is our own

when we find it, plays us
as his instrument.

He played Dante,
singing him. He played Will

like Ariel played with cause
and effect. He sang the voice

of Shakespeare without
uttering a word different

from the master's script.
He even sang through me,

played my feral well-polished
self, went spelunking in me,

singing echoes as the bats
flooded the twilight sky.

He's played through all of us,
believing in him or oblivious

of him. Nothing matters
but the music released

when he plays the instruments
of our selves, known only to us

when he we hear him sing
with our own voices and we know

the Orphic mind
isn't us.

MYTHS ARE LONG
words, definitions

of a state of being
and its potential.

Orpheus, as a myth,
means sublime

persistence. Nothing
could stop him singing.

He turned everything
into poems. That is

the essence of what
it means to be a poet.

Everything, anything,
can be transformed,

can transcend itself
into a poem—the easy

joy of a summer morning,
the catastrophe

of grief, the tragedy of
dismemberment

in depression, paranoia,
and psychosis, the mournful

severing of mind from world
which turns grief into prophesy.

Orpheus cannot be
who he is not. And he is not

a thing without poems.
Poems are who he is,

what he does with what
he knows, senses, endures.

THE PATRON OF DISCOVERY,
Orpheus models insight

as grace. Whether whispering
to Homer, or voicing

the god of order and beauty,
Orpheus allows understanding

not by trying, not by
hypothesizing, but by

listening, by being a conduit
with no baffling for the voice

beyond him and unimaginably
far above me. Discovery is

as much about opening
as it is about finding.

What is found by you
makes itself into a form

you cannot recognize
or search for, but gives

itself to you like you
give yourself to the hidden

door in the garden and slip
inside, out into a paradise

that breathes a poem into
someone else's ear.

To open yourself is a gift
from behind the door. When it

happens, you cannot help
it from happening, any more

than Orpheus could stop
himself from singing.

WHY IS ORPHEUS
an adventurer?

Is it his role as an Argonaut,
his task to deflect the horrors

of imagination—Sirens cooing,
rocks crashing and crushing—

to disarm the terrors of the stories
we inflict upon our emptiness

at night? Orpheus is the
soother of the torments

of pioneering, the calmer
of wild seas and navigator

of the straits and ragged shores
he sings. He sings meaning,

he means, and when
we hear, our demons

are set aside, pushed back
like the sides of a path

through a stormy sea parted
and safe. He makes discovery

possible by mellowing
the terrors of the void

from which all new things
emerge, reveal themselves

like comets out of the blue,
a mystery Orpheus makes human

and so makes possible for us
to accept the gift of more

from the eternal
unknown of chance,

of what is not yet, the mother
monster of all fearfulness.

ORPHEUS THINKS.
His mind makes ideas

out of metaphors.
Metaphors are what

the world understands,
relating *this* and *that*

to *that* and *this*, making
something new from two

old things that understand
each other in a way that

makes a third thing, gives
birth. Is metaphor a

dialectic without opposites?
Is that what delights the birds

and beasts and trees so much
they float together in a musical

swirl because they are moved
to do so? Is that what the

Orphic voice is saying in
countless new ways, every

which way it can?
Is that what moves you?

An inward dance
of being

gotten, met, welcomed,
seen, felt, moved? Is that

why Orpheus moves the world
to dance for joy—because it's

moved by the beauty
of his attention?

ORPHEUS THE HEALER
saved my life

from the slow suicide
of one purposeless day

after another. Saved
my life by giving me

a full
life to live,

to be lived fully,
through the calling,

the Orphic voice
that, once I started

saying it,
has never stopped

having even me
as an instrument

to play
my whole life long,

calling me to practice,
practice, practicing

wholeness, even.
I would not be eighty-three

without his
indwelling. Sanity

would have
misplaced me.

I would not
be functional, much less

alive, without him
welcoming me, rustic

that I am, into the choir,
the constellation

of selves
he still plays.

Only he could have
saved me, only he

could have charmed me
out of my stubborn

fear
of being free.

WHEN ORPHEUS SINGS
language is no longer

a separate layer
of reality, no longer

a foggy lens you can't
clear up. Language is,

with him, how nature
thinks, how rocks

cogitate, birds
originate ideas,

beasts learn melody
and tempo. It is not

some tawdry, bungling
prop to be jettisoned

as fast as breathing
in and out can do it.

Orpheus shows worldly
things what they feel

is a password to their
privacies, that they

have them at all. He
gives them voice

through his voice as
it plucks the ear

of death and says,
Did you take her back?

WHEN ORPHEUS SAVES YOUR LIFE
you are rescued by being given

a life
to live. A life

of practice, effort,
constant trying,

constant being
present, being

open, greeting
the page. It is

an act of reverence,
this practice, this

life to live, an act
of devotion,

continual thanks
for continual surprise,

for revealing,
though my pen,

the Orphic voice
within me, healing

the separation between
me and the mystery

of generation, which
has blessed my living

since I first started
trying to say what

was to be said that day.
It is impossible not to feel

the presence of more
than you are when you see

ink words start flowing
from your pen, ideas

you have, but only
after they have

been written. This is the
devotion to the More

cloaked in Orphic myth, a
story we still believe

because we live it,
live it out ourselves

in our own fragile
and indelible way.

OF ALL THE HOLY
figures, yours is

the one of most
restraint. The paradox

of extreme order
fueled by exuberance

has a consequence that
moves the earth.

It is Apollo's principle
at work in you—order

leading to beauty,
the one and only

set of opposites that
co-exist as a generative

singularity. Orpheus as
poet is the god

of order and meaning, each
dependent on

the other. The most
beautiful of all is that

which praise inspires,
the need for more order

out of beauty, the tangible
out of the ineffable. This

is why Orpheus is the first
craftsman, maker of gardens

and poems, songs and musical
proportions, tempos, speeds,

words and their sounds combined
to make the beauty of meaning

that transcends both them and
the art of perfect joinery.

THE WAY THE WORLD IS,
the way we perceive it,

Orpheus so beautifully makes
perception and reality

the same thing. Identical,
no difference. Even if we can't

hear him, he sings and the world
comes together, the trees feel

known, understood, so do
the cliff sides, fawns, giraffes,

the condors soul-hunting
in the stratosphere. That's why

Orpheus makes the world
happy, makes life and stone

dance for joy. That's why
hawks listen to him, sharks

stop snapping and feel his melody
like a new current caressing

their hunger. Orpheus understands.
The world feels understood. Praise

is compassion, clarity a kind of
sympathetic magic of affection.

[Even the wife's double death,
even that is seen for what it is,

an error in giving up,
a use of force looking back

so all love
is lost.]

IT IS A WAY OF LIFE,
a life to live, a practice

that perceives,
guides, and forms—

this Orphic
voice that

wants us to
speak it, to live

up to it, live up
to ourselves

and ourselves
in our lives. It

anchors and
gives purpose

to how we live our days,
to what we do with who we are.

Orpheus joins
Apollo god of medicine

and music, joins Athena
goddess of crafts and war

with Dionysus who rules
the proscenium world

in requiring daily devotion,
even down to running the scales,

constantly drawing, practicing
the piano, rehearsing your part,

learning even how to dance, play,
win. Orpheus wants you to work out,

stay in shape, be at the top
of your game when he comes

to sing through you,
his peculiar instrument.

He is a god. He plays
language through us all.

ORPHEUS WENT AGAINST
his early promise

of knowing by praising.
If only he had turned

his praise on himself,
trusted his place, not

doubted. If only he had been
the object of his own rejoicing,

giving himself over to his
passions and genius for joy,

let the world love him,
know him like he had loved

and known it, right-brain
magician, singing in

the language of the world,
the language that only we

cannot sense and feel as
instruments of the god,

but not the speaker nor singer
who says what only the

world without us understands.
If only he could have done the same

with his grief, given it a home,
accepted it, instead of trying to

erase it. If only he had known
to be true to himself, through

and through, this god who is
only part god, only a hybrid

imperfect as the world itself
is holy and divine.

YOUR CONSTELLATION
is a mark on the map

to the secret life of making
new things, the life nobody knows

but you, nobody, not even other
denizens foraging in that ultimate

and private realm, not even you
when you leave the room

and lock the door behind you.
Only you know how you feel

when you see words and meanings
appear from the nib of your pen,

words that weren't there
before you put them there

and hoped they would make sense
to you and might even surprise you.

They didn't come from somewhere else,
yet they appear to you like someone else's

work, not that you don't mean
what they say, you do, it's just

you didn't know what you had to say
until you said it, until you saw

what showed up. That must be
how it felt to the first Orphic voice,

singing Apollonian rhapsodies
like love songs in the shower.

EMOTION

1. Intimacy

You can tell her
anything
and her love for you
wants to hear it.
And she can say
anything to you
and is greeted by
your open heart,
like hers. And your love
for her and hers for you
prevents you both
from saying
cruel half-truths
that cannot be
explained or refined
or expanded
but are like a goathead
thereafter in your shadow.
It's all her
and the us
she makes
possible for us,
all her and me
now opening
like a vault
too big for anyone
to open
by themselves.
And the last thing
to embarrass us
as the vault door
moves with its
own weight is

the utter truth,
it is so far
at the end of the list
it has dropped off
like a robe
which shows us both
our nakedness
without us knowing
that we are
any different.

2. Delight

Something
comes about,
the source
matters little,
and you find
yourself
grinning,
your whole
body softening,
your eyes squinting
with intensity,
a joy breath
issuing from you,
some pressure easing,
our hands and even
your feet loosening.
The something
becomes for a moment
your entirety
and you reach
to cup a baby's cheek,
to feel a smoothness,
draw the iris to you
to gently gasp
intoxication as you would
point and exclaim
at a geode
opening into paradise
with the welcoming
blow of a hammer.

3. Glee

Over across
the restaurant
in a far sharp
corner, Dad
is making spit
bubbles
with his lips
so Henry
and his noodles
will chortle with
automatic zest
that changes
the whole tone
of the universe.
From that corner,
novas pale
into pink
holes of dusky
pleasure, comets
spurt milk
across the galaxy.
From that corner,
Henry has
giggled a tsunami
into a spa
with Aphrodite
dangling out
her legs so all
the warmth
of all the suns
can touch her
ankles. From
that corner,

from that wild
crinkly grin
and whoop,
the whole cosmos
leans back
and folds its hands
across its chest
and basks in
baby grace,
filling the void
with what pleases
everything there is.

4. Gratitude

You know the imp
of the perverse rides
the magic carpet
of chance, and so
you say to her
your thanks in
every way you can,
to the gods,
to change,
to the forces of time,
to the will
of the Cosmos
that drives everything
in directions
they never expected,
and never, never
check the gift horse
of good fortune
for hoof rot
and halitosis,
but always remember
how it might have gone
how you feared it would,
and how it didn't.

5. Grief

A fastidious
heaviness
up and down
the spine,
in the life ways
of the lungs,
a light-headed leaden fog,
something dear to you
in yourself pulled,
unfairly free,
into a clammy void,
swelling and pushing
ecstasy abandoned
to a corner too
remote and convoluted
to explore, a dead weight,
a ballast of harm
setting you to tip
over helplessly and spill
yourself with no
relief left behind,
the shadow moving on
without a backward glance
at life, the little door
of paradise slamming shut
with the roar of a bank vault
snapping closed with you inside,
nothing left now
but the hollow terror
of nothing left
but you.

6. Dread

You have to do it.
There's no way out.
You even want to do it.
But you can't escape.
You're caught. And
what if you flop, what
if you don't cause
elation, what if you
flub so much you
dishonor yourself and
the memory of those
you serve? That's the
black hole you must
never look into. Look
yourself straight in the eye,
right up until the first
utterance comes as you
move your lips
to speak. And then
the dread reappears
with each hard word
making them harder,
and then it's all
over and the dread
is seen for what it was,

a ludicrous waste
of imagination. You
soften it by saying
it might be the oil
of a good performance,
but humiliating waste
is not a lubricant.
And you gag on your own
foolery going down the
wrong pipe so
you are caught by
your own thoughtless
habits of fear again. Again!

7. Relief

To loosen your grip,
open your fist,
let what you had
fall away, let go,
give up, all
tension dispersing
like fog
in the sun.
The fear wall
crumbling at
the base
when your what-ifs
are declared
happily off the wall
and dismissible
with the wave of a hand,
a lift of one side
of your lip. Gone
like a train speeding off,
or an angry man
not nailing you
as the prankster
who threw a rock
at his windshield
because his rage
made him colorblind,

and he just knew the brat
was wearing red and white
and you, looking down,
saw only green and blue.
The inner phew was like
standing a foot away
from where the tsunami
finally petered out
two miles from shore.

8. Loneliness

The loneliness of longing
and the loneliness of loss
are not the same. Longing
can be healed, loss
is the presence
of finality, it exists
not to exist.
No light escapes,
nothing heals,
nothing replaces
the fathomless
absence.
It can recede from view,
from memory even,
for a while, but
it is never filled up,
it only deepens
and darkens
even as it fades
from time.

9. Contentment

Nothing
more, sweet
enough,
perfect
smooth as
bird heads,
cloud seas,
sun health,
the eager glee
of tongues
from blond dogs
who feel
your cooing
and cascade
into a holy state
of wanting
the perpetual
more
of what
is always
theirs
forever.

10. Exhaustion

It's a state,
a condition, and
an emotion—to be
played out, shot,
reduced to exhaust,
to be so thin
your will
cannot override
the vacuum
left of you.
You are becalmed,
bruised, black and blue static,
not at peace, not at all
calm, a fidgety depletion,
an achy lull. You are
that nervous emptiness
gone too far to even want
to make any sense
of anything, yet knowing
mutely there is still
sense to be made, but
right now, it'll just
have to wait, no way
to reach for it, no way
even to want it.

11. Anxiety

Cemented, feet too heavy
to run, bad breath window draft
chilling and gnawing,
every shadow lurking
with something
ominous but so
impossible, if it actually
happened to you
you couldn't believe it
when you have to pull
the harpoon out of your leg,
or start dreading
your own demise
foretold by an odd speck of skin,
or a slight wheeze, or a hitch
in your back that suddenly
brings the whole
curtain crashing down
from the proscenium,
erasing your
consciousness
from the stage
while your corpse plays
there's no business
like show business and
the show
must go on.

12. Starting

When nothing
is left behind,
it's all ahead.
But how to be
so clean and over?
So absolutely
done there's nothing
left, nothing left
at all but the open
and waiting,
the thrill of it,
heading out
into the empty
the first time,
everything
out there, waiting
to show you
there is a way
to recast the past
so it leads
to a different now,
to make it finally
work, smooth
and consistent,
"regular" in fact
without monotony,
tinkering with time,

to fill it with
the unforeseen,
the longed-for,
first and last
chances
with worlds
in between,
the wide open
all yours,
nothing in your way
but you and you've
left him preaching
to potatoes
on the side of the road.

13. Despair

Despair is no good,
of course. It gets nowhere.
It puddles, stagnates.
Grows pests that cause
collateral pain, and flailing
worries that further sink
all boats. Despair is
a door jamb. It is meant
not to budge, cement blocks
tied to the suicide's feet.
It is the end of striving,
and like a tell-tale lump
in a garden snake's body,
despair is by its nature
all over, and nothing else,
digested as far as the eye
can see, only a curiosity,
a morbid spectacle with no
known use other than
its end without ceasing.

14. Pessimism

A dead end
that engulfs you,
a no way out,
trapped
in ankle jaws,
or in a deep
pit with sharp
stakes, one
of them in
your leg, and
you muffled
and aching, and
predicting your
own end, betting
on it in fact,
helplessly realistic,
impossible, belonging
to the universal DNA
of never being
anything else
but no.

15. Resentment

It's too romantic
to call it a
simmering, even
a slow burn, but
that nagging, hang-
nail disappointment
has become so
infected and inflamed
to bump it, even
slightly, is to send
spasms of sad anger
and disbelief searing
into rage reaction,
while the pain
throbs on, keeps
jagged. It's not a
hate, not really
an anger, but a boil
you can't avoid, unless
you stand all day, which
you come to resent
even more.

RIO GRANDE ELEGIES

IT IS A VANISHMENT.
All the house habits
are gone with the house:
the checking to make sure

that no cat has slipped out,
that the alarm is disarmed,
that all the hoses are off
in the garden, that she who is

receding hasn't fallen out of bed
or slipped on the hard tile
bathroom floor. The ways
of the place: how fast the living room

heats up from the wood stove,
the black ice spot near the front steps,
the Christmas Eves with heart-friends
cheek to cheek in the tiny old kitchen,

lights from the tree caroling, wine
flowing, luminarias glowing,
good will overcoming long-ago
disappointments layered as scars

of the season. But that was another
vanishment ago when the old house
was still alive and had not been erased
by money and dreams of big spaces.

Photos now salve the losses,
and vanishments become old homelands
themselves, myth-tales spinning
an endless new ending keeping you alive.

THE OLD GARDEN
is a lost garden now.
The cat graves are
in the realm of the so

deeply forgotten they
exist only as the bottom
shadows of ideas. The
graves of human ashes

won't exist for the buyers.
One of the sacred rocks
from her grave cairn came
with me in my pocket along with

a birthstone amethyst
crystal from her sister's
disheveled shrine. The past
is now only in my recollection,

imagination sweet and fierce
as snow melt churning slow
and icy down acequia depths
in a cool, breezy late afternoon,

protected like color on primrose
blossoms, Maximilian's
ferocious green refusing
not to break out and up

through rocky soils, the last
geography of countless springs rising up
sun-bound and beyond on the fertile
ashes of days with no traces but me.

WE CAN BE HOMESICK
only for the homes
we're forced to leave.
We long for the peace,

the peace of the familiar,
the comfort of knowing
where everything is
when we need it.

We love what is lost, homes
we have left, like we miss
dead friends. The gone place
I miss most has been missing

for more than a quarter
of a century now, the old farm
house with its three-foot-thick
adobe walls, its dark cool suffusing

through the summer, its relieving
warmth at Christmas, the mind dancing,
the soul laughing, the tangoing
of serious and troubled lives

that went on there daily
in its nurturing, sturdy,
dilapidated truth—it endured
and we endured within it,

our maturity gestating there,
forming itself from the code of our lives
lived as best we could, fresh born
every day with every new conversation.

SHE TOOK IN THE TREES
on her walks, the circus
of green, the honeysuckle,
silver lace vine, the low

hanging crab apples, trumpet
vines, grapes, the whole
rainbow of green in the valley
on acequia paths, even

the green frogs sunning
on the banks and stones
among the weeds, the tall grasses.
Even the searchlight heat

of the sun gave her a new
effulgence of green light
through the leaves. She was
always there with the green

and growing edge of our green
hearts, our loving imaginations
building us farther and fuller,
flowering green morphing into reds

and peach and sage. She was
a spring form all her life, when gray
rage and cracked sorrow didn't
leave her limp with grief for lost hope

and the door that was closing on the garden.
The worst moment we ever knew together:
"I can't take you out anymore, sweet one,
I'm so sorry. I'm too weak to get you back in."

POEMS, BOOKS, COLUMNS,
studies, my collections, they
are a resistance, my acts
of subverting the crippling norm.

The land, the water, the stratigraphy,
the stones, gravel, trees, the weeds
even, are a lost horizon I admire,
hidden in their depths, helpless

myself without my love of them,
my grateful obsession with them.
They are the shadows, the deep sweet
soft corners of unconscious groves

where imagination echoes and escapes
into its pure freedom, being who we are,
our resistance every day, the cosmos itself
as it is in us, in our ant shadows of totality.

ON THE DAY THE WORLD CHANGED
you and I were three months back
from Florence, Rome, Paris and Oxford,
back from the delicious interviewer

winking at me while questioning the famous
jazz genius in the Luxemburg Gardens.
You sixty me sixty-one, in our prime, fourteen years before
you began losing your way, your wedding rings,

forgetting gin rummy, not knowing how
to comb your hair, button your shirt
or boil water without burning down the kitchen.
And now, as of yesterday, when the Roman copy

of Hermes came to live under the big pinion
thunder cloud on the new land, that whole world
of ours is as gone, as displaced, as finished off
as Nazi-occupied Paris but with no tears of relief,

as mummies curled in Vesuvian ash,
as finished as the nightmare fall
of the man and the woman holding hands
mid-air having leapt from a twin tower,

eighty stories up to escape the flames they never
dreamed of facing an hour before, buttering
their toast above the skyline over breakfast,
admiring the city at peace far below.

TOO IMPATIENT TO BE A GOOD
maker of soil, a gardener that plants
find comforting and mothering
—I used to be that, but always in a slowing

down, healing mood. We used to weed
together, taking a file to sharpen the edges
that would nick the goathead stems, and she was
always just that much more thorough

and complete. But those gardens are all
lost gardens now, gardens of memory.
And I join now with my hand adz and hoe
the ghost gardeners of Chaco or in Tano

province, patiently moving and packing
soil to just the right incline to move
water without damage. I am too old
to be impatient, my hands hurt too much

to move fast or surely, but they still work
and move soil slowly and with conscience
but homesick for when they didn't ache
and muscles and lungs could keep up

with the seasons and never fall behind.
That is the lost gardener I am, but I am still here,
still an admirer of green and proud of the green
I can nurture and the work the earth loves me to do.

EVEN DEATH HAS CHANGED.
It used to be that when you died
you were dead. Now you can
live in remission, restored

to life by luck and technique,
by human fiddling so graceful
and adroit you can be kept
going by a machine the size

of a tape measure, sturdy, reliable,
corkscrewed into your heart
with a battery that lasts so long
you could outlive it at ninety-three.

It makes thinking ahead difficult,
puts ambition in its place, makes you,
forces you to live day by day after day
with no tomorrow and all the tomorrows

you could hope for and far, far more:
what you do with them, for instance,
and where you want yourself to go.
You are alive but your energy isn't

as reliable as your pacemaker's battery.
Are you more than a leftover?
What does it mean to be alive
right now in a world you would not

be seeing, or feeling, that would
not have been there, period,
if your time had truly been over and had
come to be what used to be called the end?

IT IS OVER TODAY. I GIVE AWAY
the land that I grew up on
for a huge profit and with hope
for a new life, land that I've

tended and watered and
weeded and nurtured for more
than fifty years, the landscape
of my poems, the site of the

courting, the living, the creating
the great core bond of my life.
I turn over the keys to it,
it is no longer mine. I no longer

live there. All its secrets and tricks,
all its habits and patterns, all its
memories, all gone now. And I
am free with the greatest love

I have known, the healthiest life
I have loved and that has loved me,
reborn, seeking wholeness now,
to be the denizen, citizen of my whole

life, completing but adding new geysers,
new accretions, new stratigraphy,
a new river bed to flow through
for as long as forever might be for me.

I CANNOT CALL IT
my patria chica anymore,
the garden I have served

for three quarters of my life.
It is beyond me, like many
physical things have become,

even long walks. I am so old,
I am looking like my gaunt old dad
the year he died.

I can hardly open a jar, and yet, I am
fathomlessly alive, ambitious, full of projects
I know I can do, though I know too I'll fall asleep

as I try. I am still who I am, even exiled
as I am from who I was and still will be.
I have a new life when most are dead

or dying off. It is the will, the going on,
the way, the will be, the will to be, the willing,
the willful joy, the willful belief in being willing.

GATHERING THE HAPPY AND HYSTERICAL
memories of her at her deadpan, wild
as a buzzard, hilarious straight-faced best,
her Miss Mouseness, her unflinching

loyalty to what made sense to her,
always on my side even when I
wasn't in the groove exactly
as she'd have it; her rolodex brain

of dirty jokes, her relishment;
the role of navigator and map
keeper and cat mother of darling
monsters: "If you weren't the best

cat that ever lived, you'd be dead"
she cooed to the incontinent tom in her arms.
Now is the time to remake
your image of her in her own

image and likeness, when she was in full
battle gear, jokes sharpened, logic
armor polished and glinting, champion
of everyone seeking the best of themselves,

champion of the best life even when
it was just out of reach but there for the taking
if you could stretch your confidence just so,
out into the fiery, ridiculous, welcoming world.

HOW COULD YOU LOSE
what can't be lost?
It doesn't happen. But it does.
The daily crossword joys

she'd do with her dad.
The cat meals and endless
cradling pick-ups; the cooing
"beeeutiful doggie" to the love-

frantic wagger; Christmas Eve throngs
of affection, childhood Christmas mornings
by the tree, present pyramids piled,
eggs and bacon sizzling; and she reading

the morning paper for hours
through the noon, clipping for me
what she knew I'd need. Her fearless
witnessing, the strength she'd

give to others just from her caring,
combing her hair over the sink
to catch the loose ones. The habits
of her solitude, her rich aloneness,

pencils, papers, rich as Durer drawings.
These cannot be lost, even when you lose them
as a witness to her beloved powers,
her dear recalcitrance, her kindly

refusal to fall into the riptide.
Her obit: "she died at ninety-three after a long
struggle with cancer" which she
did not lose, nor her character

nor integrity along with her altered mind.
Her whispering to me her benediction, "You are
the kindest man I know," said to soften our guilt
at being just helplessly human.

I'VE BEEN EXILED BY DEATH
from the best friends of my life,
all of them—father, mother, wife,
brothers in spirit, all of them,

the Lake Ring people, comrades
in puzzlement, confidants, people
who knew not only who I was
but who I'd dreamed up to become

if my luck and stamina held up,
people who stood with me,
hanging on to the rudder of my
own definition of myself, people

I trusted never to betray anything
I said to them, who never took
offense at slips of the tongue—
they are all a stand of aspen

killed off by drought, beautiful
still even in the disappearance
of their living core, beautiful even
as driftwood still standing.

THE GIANT, GREAT COTTONWOOD,
stupendous in its indispensable
shade, the enormity of its body,
its tree-sized limbs, its reach

into water stretches to the four-wing
salt bush horizon and beyond,
the mushrooms growing from its lower limbs,
some amputated after a storm dropped

one of them, a whole tree-sized limb,
without hitting a thing. This tree doubled
in size over the fifty years I groomed and
tended it; it had a few remaining kin

scattered over the valley, marvels of longevity
in full strength holding up a million leaves;
one "stood in the way" of progress and was
hacked to the ground where I cross a bridge

that seems like a mild bump in the road,
a bridge I bitterly opposed with an army of others
but now use every day. Its kin, my Alamo,
now in the charge of others' hands. Sensitive hands?

Careful hands? Change is a god that can't
be channeled like a road to anywhere. We can
only witness, only hold our breath, only
give in to the implacable what-is.

IT DOESN'T COMPUTE,
mourning the loss
of one's sense of gloom
and corruption, and

tasks impossible to
perform beyond marginal
failure. They are gone
for the moment.

The troubles of the world
are out the back door and across
the ocean far, far away behind
a gate in a wall, the ends of which

cannot be known. This is all
the stuff of supreme
good fortune and privilege
no one deserves, few know

even briefly, and fewer still
seek and find. It's impossible
to pursue what you don't know
is there. But here I am

a widower, on the brink of
poverty again, grieving
the trauma of witnessing
someone I adore lose their

mind like some giant sanding
away whole mountains, leveling
them flat. Here I am, alive,
healthy enough, in love, loved,

loving, making a poem, with
enough money to live on
for a while longer. So what if it is

all built on a trap door
that could spring open
at any moment, not yet, though,
and I'm not jumping up and down either.

YOUR LOSS OF FEAR
can't be mourned,
nor your freedom
from the pain of rejection,

nor the stingy itch
of anger disappearing. As
the wise one says: No one
should neglect their studies

in the school of pain
with its full curricula
from guilt to shame
to homesickness and

the crippling of grief.
But you can't grieve
your lost nimbleness,
your aerial youth

like we grieve lost love;
that would be like grieving
the loss of a rainy day,
or cold snaps killing apricot buds.

The school of pain
teaches us to endure
the unendurable. It has
almost nothing to tell us

about the modesty of change
as our examined lives
become maps to the peace
of the familiar.

KNOWING YOUR SELF THROUGH AND THROUGH.
Does that help you know the world,
seek wholeness, and understand
the cosmos, the human tragedy,

glory and dilemma? Does knowing
one small thing lead to knowing
the probabilities of everything else?
Is that why the examined life is

the only one worth living, why
knowing thyself is the ultimate
task and salvation? When you
throw in the towel searching for

truth and reality, of ever knowing
them, losing the fight you picked
with ignorance, interior chaos,
unreflective existing, what's left

but love and trust? They are not
consolation prizes, not the crutches
of defeat. If you can grasp
the invisibility of trust, you are

no longer blind to the truth of love:
Love her, love the world through her.
That's why's morality is the icing
on the cake of aesthetics, why it's morally

unpleasant to blow your brains out
and nobody's business if you drift off
by declining to eat or drink.
The loss of innocence

is regained by doing unto yourself what you would do
in your best and highest state to another
in anguish and misery. Grief at the loss
of the will to live teaches us that

the pitiful and the merciful are mercifully
not the same. She just couldn't keep going.
So she left in the best way she could, with enough
will left to be mercifully gallant, loving and kind.

TEACHING—A GIFT I CAN NO LONGER
accept: no students. You can't play
Lady Macbeth in the bathroom mirror.
The art of it depends on a roomful and is

about giving away the power bestowed
upon by you by age, gender, place, assumed
learning and esteem, then accepting it back,
lowering your eyes when students see

you give them the head to go where they want
as they want and to say what they feel as they
feel it without wincing at the prospect of being
humiliated by power they can't withstand.

Not being able to do that anymore
is a loss you can bear if students have
always outgrown you and you have
always outdone yourself with attention.

A LIVING HUMAN SELF, ALIVE IN A WHOLE WORLD,
in a whole universe I know by hearsay mostly,
a universe, universes unimaginable, all together
in the state of being everything, nothing left out,

nothing of which I understand in a way I could
explain. I know who I am by what happens to me
and by how I respond, and by the thoughts I have
and the desires I seek to fulfill. I knew my late wife

and comrade-in-arms that way, by her behaviors, which
must in some way reflect her being. But I know too
she was more, much more than her effects, and if she is
so I must be too. That is the loss we all suffer,

the innocent sense of just being who we are, alive in a world
we can see and know. Now we know almost nothing
but fragments scattered over time, fragments we can't
keep track of, puzzles we have no hope of completing.

She is dead, I was dead but now alive, my old friend
is dead, was murdered after a long life of doing good to atone
for a murder he committed when he was nineteen, a murder
he kept secret, a murder he was "pardoned" for

because he was smart and educated himself in jail,
a murder he might have been murdered for. But
we know he is dead, once alive living with a crime,
a behavior, and effect of who he is, that he could not

endure and worked his whole life fruitlessly to erase,
and had erased for him when his whole being was
erased by the merest chance shot, stabbed, garroted
or squeezed by the strangling webs of the non-
        existent fates

that wise old people say and mean do not, cannot exist.
And I say, once again, there but for the grace of God
go I, the God that must exist. Who can make this
        stuff up?
We are more than our effects.

FOUR OF THEM, NOT MUSKETEERS BUT WILD
doers of life to the edge of the end—
a Zen thinker committing non-thinking;
a cowboy historian soldier too Catholic

to be content with booze and merely knowing
his neuroses; a wizard posing as a magician
who fangled and gamed the language
into merry flings; a scholar bum, hobo

genius hanging out in our boxcar minds
waiting to be unpacked—all of them
dead cold gone, all of them surviving
the trenches of youngness with me,

shell-shocked by the horrors of the
truth that sooner or later broke through
innocence like rabid wolves snarling
in the fog. All drinkers, smokers, girl

lovers, sad sacks, brothers trusted
to honestly want who I was to be,
who I was, trusted me to be
who I am in the field of chance

where all of us roamed without keeping track
or making report, where all of us learned
about the inside of minds so like ours, yet so unalike,
that we wanted to think our ways home, wanting

the truth as much as we thought they did
without understanding what the truth might mean
to them, a cosmic bond in the riddle of desire
wanting so much more than way too much.

THE DEAD ARE DEAD.
The bond with them is broken.
Intimacy may be a useful fantasy,
but a fantasy, little more.

They are gone but their presence
in you, their effects
in your habits and beliefs, and in
the moral second guessings

of your inner sense of what is right
and what is not, still grow in you
as old good habits and adapt themselves
to you, to new people you come to love.

You lose them but you never
lose how you were with them
and how you are now without them,
remade again, forced like a bulb

by tender luck to release
your green heart again
into the weather and its familiar,
mysterious gospel of chances.

THE ELEGAIC MEMORIES,
not grieving, but the longings,
the banks of recollection,
ideal family picnics, Christmases,

feasts, moments alone
staring into a house full
of love and cheer with a drink
outside in the dark, thinking

I belong there with them,
in the midst of that idyllic
good cheer. I am in fact
central to it, a gravity,

a magnet because I love it,
recalling the first moment
you spoke something true
to your father, your mother's

casual affectionate kiss
on your cheek which warms you
to your core, the sense
of charmed fulfillment

when you first loved being alone
in a strong blue sunny breeze
on a Saturday morning
starting out for the beach.

THE TERROR OF ABANDONMENT,
of being tossed out, chucked, thrown away,
excluded, like she was by her own
brains and her deranged brother,

suffering the greatest fear, the deepest
wound, the gravest emotional sin.
She was always terrified, not
of abandonment, but of abandoning,

being the one who tosses someone else away.
At the heart of most needy love lurks
the terror of suddenly being turned on,
tossed out the window, having crossed some line,

some trip wire that finds you on the other side
of the mirror gazing out onto the blank cold world
into which who you are has somehow delivered you.
It's our lost childhoods in a wink; no mourning that.

HE LOOKED LIKE A HOMELESS
hobo, a mythological coot in
furry slippers scuffling up
city streets, shopping bags

full of special documents and letters
and manuscripts and, if you looked,
envelopes over-stamped to be
mailed to exotic people in esoteric

places. He'd sometimes acknowledge
your help with a gift of cat food
coupons, heavily creased from
being wadded in his wallet, their

use-by date, of course, long
expired. But some of us knew
that the toothless old man gumming
his green chile cheeseburger

was a genius, a man fluent
in the world with more Latin
and Greek and savvy than most
professors of this and that,

a poet with a gift for friendship,
a learned survivor of his own worst
instincts, an old widower who bore
the tragic loss of his youth all

his long life, homeless from death
but seeking the home of his mind,
and his briefcases stored with various
confidants in various houses,

carrying one himself as he worked
the kitchens and lost his way
day after day after year after year,
finally dying face down on a rug

all alone in rooms he scrapped up,
his papers and marginalia unread,
his library tossed by a relative who
found fivers stashed between its pages.

SHE WAS THE FIRST LOVE MIRACLE,
the first moonstone woman, the first
erotic tsunami, the first great
painful passion that wouldn't heal,

the great symbol of being taken,
called by the spirit of another, by
the smile of the Madonna,
the smile of one whose peace is in

your pleasure in each other. And now
she's five years dead, a decade older than me,
a corpse when I am not, long gone, long,
long gone and over, after I learned

what happened to me did not happen to her
for long, but she was the first proof
of the truth of being overwhelmed by the life
of another, the first but not the most intense.

That's been saved for the last years
by the grace of chance, in the service
of life's greatest gift: mutual desire,
reciprocal affection. With never a doubt,

a question, a reason;
you both win it all,
that's it. Nothing less.
There *is* nothing more.

HE WAS THE GREAT MODEL OF FUN,
of how to do a happy, honest life
without comparison, and was,
at the same time, a dark model

of false guilt and self-defamation,
a man who saw sentiment as
entrapment, a man drunk
with dissatisfaction, the model

of who and what I never wanted to be
and strove with all my feral wile
to evade. He was the great shadow
blotting out everything. And yet

he was the man I knew I wanted to be,
in my own way—lavish with affection,
generous above all, a spend-thrift with
appreciation, not missing a thing

that the gods sent his way. The Janus
role model to welcome all out;
to avoid at all cost. He's still with me,
though gone long enough to be all over,

but never gone in my loathing of rumor
ice cold with supposes and the black
magic of finding your whole life missing,
instantly replaced, erased by an image,

your whole existence wiped
from the board by the mere
uttering of your own name
which is the same as his.

SHE LOVED ME WITH ALL
she had and with all kinds of
strings, all kinds of adhesions,
scar tissues, needs. She

loved me to her bones and I always
knew it. Mother love: healthy?
unhealthy? "Any love is best," as I
said long ago, describing

the source of endurance,
self-assurance, un-
solicited self-confidence
and long-term calm.

Any love is best, not "even"
hers, but hers too. I am
her son, her single loyalty.
She even forgave me

when I "left her" for my father
though I never did, coming back
every week to make sure she was
more than just skin and bones. She even

forgave me for telling her, when I
was fourteen, that I hated her when she tried
to stop me leaving, drunk with grief,
that I hated her for her drinking,

her madness, her suicidal binges,
which could, of course, never be
true. She set the tone and boundary
of how to honestly love and give

yourself to someone else.
When she died I felt her cool hand
in a smooth heavy rock holding down
a pile of poems, the first love

I trusted, gone.
It took a rock
to show me
who I truly am.

NINE MILLION SOLDIERS
killed in World War One, twenty-one million
wounded, many millions
of civilians gone. Sixty or is it

ninety million killed in World War Two?
World grief can't even
start to count it. Almost
all indigenous America

slaughtered, the carnage
of Mao, Stalin, Pol Pot, Pinochet,
the millions in Vietnam and Guatemala.
Where do we begin? Where

do we start to mourn
the look in all those eyes,
the lives who died their
own particular dreaded

death, who were tortured
into their graves, eyes of
the bodies ravaged by flood,
the look of people on the eightieth floor

as they jumped to avoid the flames?
The centrality of loss, of useless
loss, of waste-fated lives like leaves—
is this a lesson worth learning?

SO POOR
nothing added
up to
nothing, no
margin, no
safe haven, no
secret stash.
So poor
a microbe
could
land
you
in the street.
You never
grieve
that loss,
but the
factual
truth of it
having been
actual
leaves
a crippling
dread deep
in the bone
that feels
so hot
you must
pretend
it's really
cold, safe
far away
in the winter
of no
where ever
again.

THE GRACE
of being seen
as a child
for who
you could
become,
that's
what keeps us
standing now,
our spines
a gift
of the insight
of others with
the power
to show us
that we are to be
so much more
than we imagined.
That's what
makes us
loyal
dog soldiers
tied
to our lives
as we know
they must
be lived,
never
retreating, alive,
as we are,
to the edge
of the end.

WE SAID
there was
an us,
a one
plus one
and a
two
who
we were.
We had two
lives, each
of us, and
our own.
Death
changed that.
The space inside
we inhabited
echoes and haunts
like the bones
of the old house
emptied of us
as we were.
The past is full
of us, and
everyone, but
that space is now
not much more
than an Atlantis,
than an alluring
rumor, dispersing
but still catching
fire sometimes even
in the rain.

WE ARE REQUIRED,
sometimes, to take
a leap
of trust,
a leap
of being
in self-
fashioning,
to take off,
literally,
and open
a new door
and step through
into a new life.
The past guides
the leap,
it seems, through
thin air,
judges
the distance
into the new.
Without the chaos
we've left behind,
the snake skin,
dead appearance binding,
resisting our escape,

without that
and without
new eyes
to see you,
there'd be
no reason
to trust,
to find
an open
door,
to leap
just as you are,
no reason.
Trust and
the abyss
come later.

WE MOURN OURSELVES
as we were, as paradise kids
in the garden we tilled
and seeded, lavishing
the lullaby of our labor,
taking lessons from
old man Mares and his tractor,
effort that made even
our sweat taste sweet.
"We grow old, we grow old,"
our garden's overgrown,
our city is an ice rink
then a molten pond,
our friends are stains
of memory. The landscape,
once as intimate
as our own feet,
is now scribbled over
with commercial graffiti,
tagged by companies
that want a sign
of their indispensable
virtue everywhere
blocking mountains, commanding
focus, the city itself a 3D
billboard of title loans,
smoke shops, car parts,
burgers, and burgers, and burgers.

Nothing is free of this
doodling, pitching, the whole
city a checkout counter
with sirens calling
for impulse grieving, last old
friends papered over,
bulging from the mindscape
like wallpapered bugs
pasted not quite
flat enough to be
overlooked as bumps,
though completely
effaced as people.

WE ARE
what we love
more than we are
what we say
and do. We are
our fascinations.
It's the wonderment
in us that
identifies us
to ourselves,
that makes us
actual as
the objects
we cherish
on our desks,
those museums
of amazements
—the Irish
marble pencil tray,
the fossil conch,
the fifth-century
Attic silver coin
with the owl
of Athena,
the Zuni badgers,
the circular
and banded stones,

the dinosaur coprolite,
the rutile in quartz,
stones from Everest
and Sinai in one
straw Chinese box,
the bronze of Hermes,
the puma skull in all
her furious perfection.
These are myth-tales
beyond translation,
understood only
in the magic glade
where love and
curiosity are mating.

I OWE MANY PEOPLE my deepest thanks for helping me survive the strange, tragic, and transformative tangle of events that overtook me from 2016 to 2020. Just before the onset of the Covid pandemic, my wife and closest friend of fifty-two years, the artist and cancer survivor Rini Price, died of complications from a five-year slide into dementia.

As the pandemic began to leave the front pages in New Mexico, an incredible gust of good fortune just days after my eightieth birthday allowed me to meet and then fall in love with Robin Swift, a profoundly wise, kind, and loving student of life whose generosity knows no bounds. Widowed some twenty years before when her Episcopalian minster husband, Bill Swift, died prematurely of cancer, Robin developed her career as a public health educator and administer working in family planning, AIDS/HIV education, and death and dying services. We have become each other's life partners and have flourished together, engaging in a profoundly open and fascinating ongoing conversation through the thickets and open meadows of our lives.

I would not have met Robin had it not been for the postmortem intervention of my closest friend, the artist and poet Skip Graham, whose death from complications of cardiac surgery served as an uncanny medium of introduction. My grief over his unexpected death was the catalyst for my first conversation with Robin at the Campo Bar at Los Poblanos Farm. Slightly more than a year after Rini's death, I experienced a complete cardiac arrest in the office of my physician Dr. Matt Slough at the UNM Senior Center. I would have died then and there had it not been for him coming to my rescue, along with his nurse Sandy Morrison and the medics of the EMT team that defibrillated me and took me to UNM Hospital where Robin was waiting and watched over me after a pacemaker was implanted.

I wouldn't have been in Dr. Slough's office in the first place if it hadn't been through the good offices of his colleague Dr. Carla Herman, Robin's friend who was head of geriatrics and my doctor at the time. Dr. Herman, her partner and our friend Dr. John Robertson, and my cardiologist Dr. Paul Andre have been enduring mainstays of consolation and good advice.

The gift of Orpheus, Rilke's *Sonnets to Orpheus* and the life-altering book by Elizabeth Sewell, *The Orphic Voice*, came to me in 1960 from the poet, translator, and magus Cecil Robert Lloyd, aka the Wombat, a homeless person with many temporary homes, who roamed the streets of Albuquerque for forty years teaching young people how to read and think clearly, including me and our mutual friend the physician Dr. Robin (Robert) George. Dr. George translated most of the ancient Greek women poets, oracles, and sybils, and was working on a long prose analysis of Asclepius, the ancient Greek god of healing, before he died prematurely. I was empowered by him to consider writing about Orpheus and was enlightened by our years of conversation in his fulsome Corrales library of ancient Greek and Latin literature and philosophy.

V. B. Price has been working, as he says, to repair his ignorance since he came to New Mexico in 1958 at the age of eighteen. He studied anthropology and philosophy at the University of New Mexico and has been publishing poetry since 1962. He's worked continuously as a reporter and an environmental and political columnist for nearly as long. His column currently runs at mercmessenger.com. He had the great privilege of teaching at UNM's School of Architecture and Planning and in UNM's Honors College for more than three decades. He received the 2021 New Mexico Literary Arts Gratitude Award for contributions to the life of the poetry community in New Mexico and the Southwest, and he has also been elected to the Board of Directors for the Leopold Writing Program.

His father once called him "fortune's child." The vast luck of his life is embodied in his children, his grandchildren, and in the landscape of his beloveds both in the ground and still walking upon it. His good fortune blossoms in the students who have mentored him, in the friends who have taught him, and in New Mexico who has mothered him.

CASA URRACA PRESS PUBLISHES creative nonfiction, poetry, photography, and other works by authors we believe in. New Mexico and the US Southwest are rich in creative and literary talent, and the rest of the world deserves to experience our perspectives. So we champion books that belong in the conversation—books with the power, compassion, and variety to bring very different people closer together.

We are proudly centered in the high desert somewhere near Abiquiú, New Mexico. Our books are available through independent booksellers everywhere. You can visit us online at casaurracapress.com for all available editions of our books and to register for workshops with our authors.